THE

GOD

CHASERS

Interactive Study Guide

**Meditative Questions for
Personal Use and Small Group Discussions**

THE

GOD

CHASERS

TOMMY TENNEY

Interactive Study Guide
compiled by

Dian Layton

Meditative Questions for
Personal Use and Small Group Discussions

Destiny Image® Publishers, Inc.
P.O. Box 310
Shippensburg, PA 17257-0310

ISBN 0-7684-2105-5

For Worldwide Distribution
Printed in the U.S.A.

Second Printing: 2001   Third Printing: 2002

This book and all other Destiny Image, Revival Press,
MercyPlace, Fresh Bread, Destiny Image Fiction,
and Treasure House books are available
at Christian bookstores and distributors worldwide.

For a U.S. bookstore nearest you, call **1-800-722-6774**.
For more information on foreign distributors, call **717-532-3040**.
Or reach us on the Internet: **www.destinyimage.com**

Contents

Publisher's Page

Run! Run! Run!

Get ready to put on your shoes and enter another adventure with
Tommy Tenney. *The God Chasers Interactive Study Guide* is an effec-
tive resource tool that will take you deeper into the many truths
you first discovered in *The God Chasers*.

Too often, we read a book and are blessed during the initial reading, but soon forget the impact it had on us. This *Interactive Study
Guide* is a starting place to leave the surface of simply reading the
book. You will be able to plunge deep into a fuller search and
application of the realities revealed in *The God Chasers*.

It will open your heart to explore again the spiritual scenery
creatively written by the pen of Tommy Tenney.

Don Nori
Publisher

Preface

The very fact that you, fellow-God chaser, are reading this book reveals that you want to know the Lord, not just know about Him.

Please, please, *please* do not approach this as another "how-to" book. As you read, be open to the Spirit of the Lord. In the midst of this study experience, He would like you to *experience* His presence!

Allow Him to catch you as you chase Him.

While you are reading *The God Chasers*, and at any other time throughout your day when you feel the slightest inkling of His nearness, stop everything and focus on Him! Press into Him. Chase Him. Lift your heart and voice to Him and welcome His presence.

At the end of each chapter we have included a "CATCH Phrase." These few words capture the basic principle being presented in the chapter—a phrase you can repeat throughout your day.

This book can be used by individuals or in a group setting.

It is our prayer that through this interactive study guide, you learn not only to chase God, but that catching Him becomes a way of life.

Dian Layton

Introduction by Tommy Tenney

I didn't really want to write a "study guide" for *The God Chasers*. Study guides and workbooks tend to be so information oriented and *The God Chasers* is more impartation oriented. No amount of information, no matter how interesting or beneficial, will make you a "God chaser." That is something that must be caught, not taught. You can study the lives of men and women whose passion for Him changed the course of history...yet remain unchanged yourself. You can read prayers and cries of saints who touched Heaven...and remain untouched and unmoved. You can gather all the information that the world has to offer...and miss the impartation that God longs to give.

But after hearing of so many who have used *The God Chasers* as a tool to teach from, and after reading letters from people in those classes, I felt that I just had to get involved.

It is my prayer that this study guide will give you something to think about in your personal devotions—that your devotions will prompt discussions in your study groups—but most importantly, I pray that they will impart hunger and spark a deeper, more intimate dialogue between you and God.

May God bless you in your pursuit.

Chapter 1

The Day I Almost Caught Him

Running hard after God–Ps. 63:8

We have studied God's Word and His old love letters to the churches so much that some of us claim to know *all* about God. But now people like you and me around the world are beginning to hear a voice speak to them with persistent but piercing repetition in the stillness of the night:

"I'm not asking you how much you know *about* Me.
I want to ask you, 'Do you really *know* Me?
Do you really *want* Me?' "

The God Chasers page 1

Chase the Key Word Through the Chapter
As you read Chapter 1, highlight or underline the key word, "know." It appears a total of 38 times. Also highlight statements that you find particularly impacting.

Ask Some Questions
1. What is the difference between knowing *about* God and actually *knowing* God? What is the difference between serving God and having a relationship with Him?

2. How did you initially get to know the Lord? How did you get to your present place of knowing Him? *I grew up in the Church, by seeking him through prayer & the Word.*

3. What does it mean to be hungry for God? What encourages people to be hungry for Him? What encourages you to be hungry for Him? *a great desire for him, being in his presence, being in his presence feeling the holy spirit tugging at my heart.*

4. What does it mean to seek God's face and not His hand? Do you seek His face every day? Why or why not? *to seek God himself, not his gifts or blessings. yes but not long enough.*

God Chaser Experience

The only way for you to get to know someone is to spend time with them. It is the same with God. Do you want to know Him, really know Him? Then you absolutely must spend time with Him. Look at your schedule for the next week. Make an appointment with God each day and mark it on your calendar or planner. Determine how long this appointment will last each day. Plan to spend at least

15 minutes. For the next seven days, make this appointment an unquestionable necessity. Don't let anything postpone or cancel your time with the Lord.

During your appointments with God this week, use the following outline to chase Him in the Word and prayer:

Chase Him in the Word—Part A
Read about the biblical God Chaser, David, in the following portions of Scripture: First Samuel 16:18-23; 30:6; Second Samuel 6:12-15; Acts 13:22 and throughout the Psalms. As you read, consider aspects of David's chase that you could implement in your own life and jot notes in the area below.

_____

_____

_____

_____

_____

Chase Him in the Word—Part B
The following Scriptures speak about chasing or seeking the Lord. Read one each day and jot brief notes of key words and thoughts in the verse(s). (Note: Also read the Scriptures that are mentioned in Chapter 1 of the book.)

Psalm 63:8

_____

_____

Psalm 42:1-2

_____

_____

First Chronicles 16:10-11

_____

_____

Second Chronicles 7:14

_____

_____

Hebrews 11:6

_____

_____

Psalm 27:8

_____

_____

Psalm 62:5-8

_____

_____

Chase Him in Prayer
Now use the Scriptures above as a prayer guide. Read each one aloud and then convert it into a prayer.

Example: Read the verse aloud
First Chronicles 16:10–11 (NIV): "Glory in His holy name; let the hearts of those who seek the Lord rejoice. Look to the Lord and His strength; seek His face always."

Pray the words you have read
"Lord, I glory in Your name. I'm seeking You right now, and I let my heart rejoice! You are so good! Today, I look to You and Your

strength. I need Your strength, Lord. I look for and seek Your face. I want to see You, Jesus. I want to know You better."

Continue in a similar manner through each verse.
Read it aloud, then make it your prayer.

Chapter 1 closes with the following statements:

The Holy Spirit may already be speaking to you. If you are barely holding back the tears, then let them go. I ask the Lord, right now, to awaken an old, old hunger that you have almost forgotten. Perhaps you used to feel this way in days gone by, but you've allowed other things to fill you up and replace that desire for His presence.

In Jesus' name, I release you from dead religion into spiritual hunger, this very moment. I pray that you get so hungry for God that you don't care about anything else.

I think I see a flickering flame. *He* will "fan" that.

Lord, we just want Your presence. We are so hungry.

The God Chasers page 16

Get Caught!

Right now, where you are, lift your hands to Him in an act of surrender to His Spirit. Don't speak. Just wait quietly and feel His nearness. Listen for His voice. (Note: God speaks many, many languages and one of His favorites is the language of pictures.)

CATCH Phrase—"I'll follow hard when life is hard!"
Most people respond to circumstances in habitual ways. Throughout the Book of Psalms, especially in chapters 61 and 91, David said he would "run to the rock" when he felt overwhelmed. Where do you run? To the refrigerator? To the mall? To some addictive substance? Try running to the Rock—to the Lord Jesus! Whenever you are faced with difficulties, problems, or major decisions this week, press toward God with all your strength. Lean into His Spirit. *Experience* chasing God in the midst of it all and allow Him to rescue you. Form a new habitual response of chasing Him in times of trouble. Repeat the CATCH phrase to yourself throughout each day:

"I'll follow hard when life is hard!"

Chapter 2

No Bread in the "House of Bread"

Crumbs in the carpet and empty shelves

> The priority of God's presence has been lost in the modern Church. We're like bakeries that are open, but have no bread. And furthermore, we're not interested in selling bread.
>
> We just like the chit-chat that goes on around cold ovens and empty shelves. In fact, I wonder, do we even know whether He's here or not, and if He is here, what He's doing? Where He is going? Or are we just too preoccupied with sweeping out imaginary crumbs from bakeries with no bread?
>
> *The God Chasers* page 17

Chase the Key Words Through the Chapter

As you read Chapter 2, highlight or underline the word, "bread." It appears a total of 73 times. Also highlight the words, "hunger" and "hungry" which occur a total of 33 times. Include in your highlighting chase the statements that you find particularly impacting. As you read, be open to the Lord. In the midst of this study experience, He would like you to *taste the bread of His presence*!

Ask Some Questions

1. What do you think it would look like if God were to "show up" in your city or town? Do people see that God has "shown up" in your life? *Today*, how can you let God "show up"?

2. Many people mistake inner hunger for the need of some kind of natural satisfaction. The emptiness we feel inside should drive us closer to the only One who can truly satisfy. When your soul is hungry, what do you tend to fill it up with?

3. Page 27 speaks about people who are starving in countries like Ethiopia. What would your church service look like if people got that hungry for God?

4. Are you hungry for more of God? *Be happy!* Jesus said in Matthew 5:6 that you are blessed—happy and to be envied—if you are hungry! He loves to satisfy the hungry heart with His presence. Are you hungry for a deeper relationship with Him? How is that hunger evident in your daily life?

God Chaser Experience

Continue to keep last week's recommended appointments with the Lord, making them an unquestionable necessity. Don't let anything postpone or cancel your time with the Lord.

This week—FAST. Choose a food item or some activity that you usually turn to for satisfaction and replace it with time getting satisfied in God's presence.

During your appointments with God this week, use the following outline to chase Him in the Word and prayer.

Chase Him in the Word—Part A

Read about the biblical God Chaser, Ruth, in the four chapters of the Book of Ruth. As you read, consider aspects of both Ruth and Naomi's lives that are relevant to your own life and jot notes in the area below.

_____

_____

_____

_____

_____

_____

Chase Him in the Word—Part B

The following Scriptures speak about hunger or being satisfied with the bread of His presence. Read one each day and make brief notes of key words and thoughts in the verse(s). (Note: Also read the Scriptures that are mentioned in Chapter 2 of the book.)

Matthew 4:4; Luke 4:4

_____

_____

John 6:35-51

_____

_____

Isaiah 55:1-2

_____

_____

John 4:31-34

_____

_____

Psalm 17:15

_____

_____

Matthew 5:6; Luke 6:21

_____

_____

Psalm 63:1; 84:2

_____

_____

Chase Him in Prayer

Now use the Scriptures above as a prayer guide. Read each one aloud and then convert it into a prayer.

Example: Read the verse aloud
John 4:34: "Jesus said to them, 'My food is to do the will of Him who sent Me, and to finish His work.'"

Pray the words you have read
"Lord, my food—the thing that fulfills my hunger—is obedience to Your will. Help me to walk in obedience to You today, and I will experience satisfaction."

Continue in a similar manner through each verse.
Read it aloud, then make it your prayer.

Father, I pray that a spirit of spiritual violence will grip our hearts, that You will turn us into warriors of worship. I pray that we will not stop until we break through the heavens, until there's a crack in the heavenlies, until there is an open heaven. Our cities and nation need You, Lord. We need You. We're tired of digging through the carpet for crumbs. Send us Your hot bread from Heaven, send us the manna of Your presence....

No matter what you need or feel you lack in your life—what you *really* need is *Him*. And the way to get Him is to get hungry. I pray that God will give you an impartation of *hunger* because that will qualify you for the promise of the fullness. Jesus said: "Blessed are they which do hunger and thirst after righteousness: for they shall be filled" (Mt. 5:6).

If we can get hungry, then He can make us holy. Then He can put the pieces of our broken lives back together. But our hunger is the key. So when you find yourself digging for crumbs in the carpet at the House of Bread, you should be praying, "Lord, stir up a firestorm of hunger in me."

The God Chasers page 32

Get Caught!

Right now, where you are, kneel in a position of submitted humility. Whisper to the Lord. Tell Him how hungry you are. Then "soak" in His presence. Allow Him to minister to your deepest longings.

CATCH Phrase—"When I feel empty, I'll hunger for God!"

Whenever you feel an inner emptiness this week, instead of resorting to your usual temporal means of satisfaction, go to the Lord.

Run into His presence. Repeat the CATCH phrase to yourself throughout each day:

"When I feel empty, I'll hunger for God!"

****

Additional Exercise: Bake Bread!

Purchase some Pillsbury bread dough and bake it in the oven during your meeting time. As the aroma causes stirrings of hunger in your stomach, compare that desire to spiritual hunger. Do you long for His presence? Ask the Lord to make you truly hungry for Him.

****

Chapter 3

There's Got to Be More

Rediscovering the manifest presence of God

I don't know about you, my friend, but there's a driving passion in my heart that whispers to me that there's more than what I already know, more than what I already have. It makes me jealous of John, who wrote Revelation. It makes me envious of people who get glimpses out of *this* world into *that* world and see things that I only dream about. I know there's more. One reason I know there's more is because of those who have encountered the "more" and were never the same. God chasers! My prayer is, *I want to see You like John saw You!*

The God Chasers page 35

Chase the Key Words Through the Chapter

As you read Chapter 3, highlight or underline the words, "manifest presence" and "presence of God." Include in your highlighting chase those statements that you find particularly impacting. As you read, be open to the Lord. In the midst of this study experience, He would like you to *actually experience the manifest presence of God!*

Ask Some Questions

1. What is the difference between the omnipresence of God and the manifest presence of God? Do you know (or know of) any modern day individuals who have had "Damascus Road" encounters with God? Have you ever had an encounter with God that forever changed you?

2. Who were some of God's favorite people in the Bible? Were they perfect? Why did God delight in them?

3. If we want God's manifest presence in our church services, what do we need to do? Where will it begin?

Chase Him in the Word—Part A

Read about some of the biblical God chasers who encountered the manifest presence of God: John, in the Book of Revelation, specifically Revelation 1:10-18; Saul in Acts 9:3-9; Uzzah in Second Samuel 6:6-7; the musicians and priests in Second Chronicles 5:13-14; and Jacob in Genesis 32:24-30. As you read, consider what your response might have been in each of their encounters, and jot notes in the area below.

_____

_____

_____

_____

_____

_____

Chase Him in the Word—Part B

The following Scriptures speak about being in His presence. Read one each day and briefly note key words and thoughts in the verse(s).

Genesis 3:8

_____

_____

Exodus 33:14-15

_____

_____

Psalm 16:11; 95:2

_____

_____

Jeremiah 29:12-14; 33:3

_____

_____

Acts 17:27-28

_____

_____

Deuteronomy 10:9; Hebrews 11:6

_____

_____

Isaiah 55:1; Revelation 22:17

_____

_____

Chase Him in Prayer
Now use the Scriptures above as a prayer guide. Read each one aloud and then form it into a prayer.

Example: Read the verse aloud
Hebrews 11:6 (NIV): "...without faith it is impossible to please God, because anyone who comes to Him must believe that He exists and that He rewards those who earnestly seek Him."

Deuteronomy 10:9 (NIV): "That is why the Levites have no share or inheritance among their brothers; the Lord is their inheritance, as the Lord your God told them."

Pray the words you have read

"Lord, I earnestly seek for You. I don't want to just go through religious exercises. I believe that You exist and I really, really want to know You. You, Lord, are the reward I seek. Reward me with Your presence."

Continue in a similar manner through each verse.
Read it aloud, then make it your prayer.

God Chaser Experience

Now that you've read about people who have had encounters with God, and now that you have studied Scriptures clearly stating God's desire to be close to His people, experience His nearness for yourself!

Get Caught!

Here is something you can try: Sit alone in your room and simply ask God to make Himself real to you. You may or may not feel His immediate presence, but know that He promises that we will find Him when we search for Him with all our hearts (See Jer. 29:13).

Sit and wait, claiming His promise. As you wait, the Holy Spirit will bring areas of your life to mind where you need cleansing and forgiveness. Whisper prayers of repentance. Cry. Tears are very healing and cleansing. Let Jesus wash your sins and your weariness away. After your meeting with Him, you will feel stronger, fresher, and cleaner throughout your being. It's a promise.

CATCH Phrase—"I'm conscious of Your Presence, Lord."
Remind yourself throughout each day that God is with you. Look for His appearing in your home, at work, during rest and exercise, and in your meeting times with Him. Pause at regular intervals and whisper:

"I'm conscious of Your presence, Lord."

The manifest presence of God often lingers in a place even when no one else is around. I remember the day a member of the church staff at a church that God invaded crossed the platform in the sanctuary on a weekday to refresh the platform water. He never made it back. Three hours later somebody noticed that he was gone and they went looking for him. The light was dim in the sanctuary, and when they turned on the lights, they saw the man lying prostrate on the platform where he had fallen after stumbling into the cloud of His presence.

The God Chasers page 39

Chapter 4

Dead Men See His Face

The secret path to His presence

"I know it's here somewhere; I can tell I'm close. There has got to be a way to get in there. Oh, there it is. This path doesn't look really nice, though. In fact, it's kind of broken and bloody. Let's see what they call this path... Repentance. Are you sure this is the way? Are you sure this is how I can reach my goal of His face and His presence? I'm going to ask a fellow traveler. Moses, what do you say? You've been there; tell me."

*And the Lord said unto Moses, I will do this thing also that thou hast spoken: for thou hast found grace in My sight, and I know thee by name. And he said, I beseech Thee, **show me Thy glory**....And He said, **Thou canst not see My face: for there shall no man see Me, and live** (Exodus 33:17-18,20 KJV).*

The God Chasers page 51

Chase the Key Words Through the Chapter

As you read Chapter 4, highlight or underline the words, "repent," "repentance," (18 times) and "death" (29 times). Include in your highlighting chase those statements that you find particularly impacting and challenging. As you read, be open to the Lord. In the midst of this study experience, He would like you to *experience true repentance and dying to yourself.*

Ask Some Questions

1. Can you think of a Bible character who needed a break-through? Where in your life do you need a breakthrough? *Often it is that very place where you need to be broken.* Brokenness to breakthrough can be a daily experience. What patterns in your life need to be broken? Repent! Die to your self and allow God to rebuild that area of your life.

2. God's logic is very different from man's logic.
    I must decrease so that God can increase (see Jn. 3:30).
    If you want to keep your life, you must lose it (see Mt. 16:25).
    If you want to be great, become servant to all (see Mk. 10:43-45).
    Have you ever faced a time of decrease in your life? How did it feel? Did you experience God's power and presence increasing in the midst of or following that time?

3. Think of a Bible character who wanted to please himself and not God. Now think about areas in your own life where you are trying to win the favor of people. In what areas are you trying to please yourself?

God Chaser Experience

At numerous places throughout the Book of Psalms, it says, "Bless the Lord, oh my soul" (Psalm 103:1,2,22; 104:1). It does not say, "Oh my Lord, bless my soul."

Far too often, we as God's people ask Him to bless us. This week, make a change in your life. Instead of asking for God's blessings, ask Him what you can do, right in the midst of daily circumstances and challenges, that would bless Him. What response can you offer that would make God really happy?

Chase Him in the Word—Part A

Read the following Scriptures about John the Baptist, God chaser extraordinaire. Make a note about each verse in the space provided.

John 3:30

_____

_____

Matthew 11:11a

_____

_____

John 3:27

_____

_____

Chase Him in the Word—Part B

The following Scriptures speak about death to self and/or living for Him. Read one each day and briefly note key words and thoughts in the verse(s).

Revelation 12:11; Exodus 33:20

_____

_____

First Corinthians 15:31

_____

_____

John 12:43; Galatians 1:10

_____

_____

John 8:29

_____

_____

Colossians 3:22-24

_____

_____

First Corinthians 6:20; 7:23

_____

_____

Romans 12:1

_____

_____

Chase Him in Prayer

Now use the previous Scriptures as a prayer guide. Read each one aloud and then form it into a prayer.

Example: Read the verse aloud

Romans 12:1 (NIV): "Therefore, I urge you, brothers, in view of God's mercy, to offer your bodies as living sacrifices, holy and pleasing to God—this is your spiritual act of worship."

Pray the words you have read

"Lord, as a spiritual act of worship, I present myself to You. I surrender my dreams, goals, and plans and give my life in its entirety to You. I lay down my own selfish desires and yield myself to Your will. I will live this moment, this day, not to please myself or other people, but to please You. Amen."

Continue in a similar manner through each verse.
Read it aloud, then make it your prayer.

Get Caught!

Lay down on the altar. Go ahead. Pick a piece of floor and lay yourself down as a visual act of surrender to God's purposes. As you lie there, allow the flame of His presence to burn up the "stuff" in your life. Ask the Holy Spirit to show you areas where you have not submitted to His will and repent from each one. When you rise to your feet, continue the same attitude of surrender throughout the day. If you feel selfish attitudes rising up within your heart, find a spot alone and lie down again! Repeat the visual act of surrender. This outward exercise will do much to bend your inner attitudes toward God's will.

> ### The more death that God smells, the closer He can come.
>
> It's as if the smell of that sacrifice was a signal that God could draw near to His people for a moment without striking them down for their sin. His end goal has always been reunion and intimate communion with mankind, His highest creation; but sin made that a fatal affair. God cannot come close to living flesh because it reeks of the world. It has to be dead flesh for Him to come close. So when we beg for God to come close, he will, but He also says, "I can't really get any closer, because if I do, your flesh will be destroyed. I want you to understand that if you will just go ahead and die, then I can come near to you."
>
> That is why repentance and brokenness—the New Testament equivalent of death—brings the manifest presence of God so near.
>
> *The God Chasers* page 60

CATCH Phrase—"I'm dying to see You, Lord."

Remind yourself throughout each day that your life belongs to Him and your words, thoughts, and actions are to please Him. Look for opportunities in your home, at work, during rest and exercise, and in your meeting times with Him. Pause at regular intervals and whisper:

"I'm dying to see You, Lord."

Chapter 5

Do We Run Away or Go In?

A chance to meet the One you always knew was there

> And ***the people stood afar off,*** *and* **Moses drew near** *unto the thick darkness where God was* (Exodus 20:21).
>
> They saw the lightning and heard the thunder, and they shrank back in fear. They ran from His presence instead of pursuing Him as Moses did. They were unhappy with the style of leadership that God had chosen. (He couldn't lay down His identity as the Almighty God just to please man then, and He won't do it today either.) So the end result of their flight from holy intimacy that day was that they died before they or their children ever entered the promised land. They preferred distant respect over intimate relationship.
>
> *The God Chasers* page 71

Chase the Key Words Through the Chapter

As you read Chapter 5, highlight or underline the words, "call" or "calling" (18 times) and "come" or "coming" (30 times). Include in your highlighting chase those statements that you find particularly impacting and challenging. As you read, be open to the Lord. In the midst of this study experience, He would like you to *answer His call to come closer.*

Ask Some Questions

1. How did God make "a people" out of the Israelites? How is God calling us to become "a people"? Do your family members and coworkers see *you* as one of God's people?

2. How do you gauge how close you are to God? Is it by the blessings you receive? By what standards should you gauge your relationship to Him?

3. Why did the Israelites run from an encounter with God? Why do we run away from God? Why are we afraid to deal directly with God?

God Chasers Deal Direct!

Many Christians run from conference to conference, from prophet to prophet, hoping to hear from God. God wants us to run to *Him*, not to other people and places.

Visual Exercise: Stand before Mount Sinai. Visualize yourself standing before God. Present yourself to Him, saying, "Here I am, Lord. I answer Your call. I want to come closer, no matter what the cost. Here I am, Lord."

As you continue to have your daily appointments with God this week, begin each meeting in this way. As you read His Word and pray, continue in the posture of presenting yourself to Him with a desire to hear directly from Him.

Chase Him in the Word—Part A
Read the following Scriptures about the children of Israel. Write notes about each text in the space provided.

Exodus 19:3-6

_____

_____

Exodus 19:10-11,13b

_____

_____

Exodus 20:18-21

_____

_____

Chase Him in the Word—Part B
The following Scriptures speak of the Lord's desire for us to be the "people of God" in close relationship to Himself. Briefly note key words and thoughts in the verses.

Exodus 19:6-7

_____

_____

First Peter 2:5,9; Revelation 1:6

_____

_____

Deuteronomy 29:13

_____

_____

Second Samuel 7:23-24

_____

_____

Hebrews 8:10-13

_____

_____

Hebrews 10:19-22

_____

_____

First Timothy 2:5 (God chasers deal direct!)

_____

_____

Chase Him in Prayer

Now use the Scriptures above as a prayer guide. Read each one aloud and then form it into a prayer.

Example: Read the verse aloud

First Timothy 2:5 (NIV): "For there is one God and one mediator between God and men, the man Christ Jesus."

Pray the words you have read
"Jesus, I'm so thankful that You made a way for me to come boldly into God's presence. You made a way for me to 'deal direct' with God. I present myself to you this day, Lord, and say, 'Here I am.' Amen."

Continue in a similar manner through each verse.
Read it aloud, then make it your prayer.

God is calling. The first time God revealed this to me, I trembled and wept in front of the people as I told them the same thing I tell you today: "You are at Mount Sinai today, and God is calling you into personal intimacy with Him. If you dare to answer His call, then it is going to redefine everything you've ever done." Your decision today will determine whether you go forward or backward in your walk with Christ.

Intimacy with God requires a certain level of brokenness because purity comes from brokenness. The games are over, friend. He's calling you.

The God Chasers page 80

CATCH Phrase—"God chasers deal direct."
Remind yourself throughout each day that you have direct access to the throne of Almighty God. Because of the blood of Jesus, you can boldly enter the Holy of Holies and make your requests known to Him. Come boldly, knowing you are a child of God.

"God chasers deal direct."

Chapter 6

How to Handle the Holy

Moving from anointing to glory

My life changed forever on the October weekend in Houston, Texas, when God's presence invaded the atmosphere like a thunderbolt and split the podium at the Sunday service. I'll never forget telling my friend, the pastor, "You know, *God could have killed you.*" I wasn't laughing when I said it. It was as if God had said, "I'm here and I want you to *respect* My presence." A picture of Uzzah's grave had popped into my mind.

We didn't know what we were asking for when we said we "wanted God." I know I thought I did, but I didn't. When God actually showed up, none of us were prepared for the reality of His presence.

The God Chasers page 83

Chase the Key Words Through the Chapter

As you read Chapter 6, highlight or underline the words, "holy" or "holiness" (32 times). Include in your highlighting chase those statements that you find particularly impacting and challenging. As you read, be open to the Lord. In the midst of this study experience, He would like you to *reverence His holiness.*

Ask Some Questions

1. How did the Israelites treat the Ark without the respect it deserved?

    In what way are we treating the holy things of God without due respect?

2. How did David first learn from his mistakes? What did he do differently the second time?

    How can we follow David's example and learn from history and our mistakes?

3. Have you ever hit a divine "bump in the road"? Did you think it was "divine" at the time?

    What speed bumps loom ahead in your road?

God Chaser Experience
Stop. What decisions are you about to make? Have you asked God what *He* wants you to do? Ask Him right now. Then listen. Let Him speak and give you direction.

Chase Him in the Word—Part A
Read the following Scriptures about the Ark of the Covenant, and the "bump in the road." Write notes about each text in the space provided.

First Chronicles 13:2-5

_____

_____

First Chronicles 13:6-12

_____

_____

First Chronicles 15:1-2, 12-13

_____

_____

Chase Him in the Word—Part B
The following Scriptures speak of the Lord's holiness. Briefly note key words and thoughts in the verse(s).

Psalm 99:9

_____

_____

Proverbs 9:10

_____

_____

Isaiah 6:3-5; 35:8

_____

_____

Revelation 4:8

_____

_____

First Peter 1:15-16; Second Peter 3:11

_____

_____

Hebrews 12:14

_____

_____

Psalm 29:2; 96:9

_____

_____

Chase Him in Prayer

After reading the verses about holiness, speak softly and reverently to God. Tell Him what you respect about Him. Tell Him everything you are not, and everything He is. Consider the greatness of the Lord and sit quietly in awe of Him.

> The crux of the whole matter is simple: Do you really want Him to come? Are you willing to pay the cost of becoming a God chaser? Then you will have to learn how to properly reverence, handle, and steward the holiness of God.
>
> *The God Chasers* page 84
>
> It used to be easy to handle the anointing, but now I know it is a sacred thing. Now I am careful to pray two things before I minister in most cases: I pray a prayer of thanksgiving first of all, saying, "Thank You, Lord, for visiting us." Then I ask the second part of that prayer, "Please stay, Lord."
>
> *The God Chasers* page 85

CATCH Phrase—"Holy, Holy, Holy."

Be like the living creatures in Revelation 4:8 (NIV). Day and night they never stop saying: *"Holy, holy, holy* is the Lord God Almighty, who was, and is, and is to come."

Remind yourself throughout each day that God is holy. When wrong thoughts try to come into your mind, speak as a declaration, *"Holy, Holy, Holy"* and resist unholy thoughts. Before you speak to anyone, pause and think about what it is you are about to say. Are your words holy and pure? Whisper to your soul, *"Holy, Holy, Holy."* Choose carefully what you speak to that family member, coworker, waitress, or salesperson...

God is awesome in wonder and power. Do not take Him for granted and do not assume that you are making right choices. Ask for His help and wisdom to make holy decisions.

"Holy, Holy, Holy."

Chapter 7

He's Done It Before;
He Can Do It Again

Send the rain, Lord!

> We want God to change the world. But He cannot change the world until He can change us. In our present state we are in no position to *affect* anything. But if we will submit to the Master Potter, He will make us—all of us—into what He needs us to be. He may remake the vessel of our flesh many times, but if we will submit to the Potter's touch, He can turn us into vessels of honor, power, and life. After all, wasn't He the One who turned unlearned fishermen into world-changers and hated tax collectors into fearless revivalists? *If He did it once, He can do it again!*
>
> *The God Chasers* page 101

Chase the Key Word Through the Chapter

As you read Chapter 7, highlight or underline the word, "rain" (19 times). Include in your highlighting chase those statements that you find particularly impacting. As you read, be open to the Lord. In the midst of this study experience, He would like to *send the rain of His Spirit to you!*

Ask Some Questions

1. What person in the Bible was very "rough," but God reshaped him or her? How were you "rough" before you knew the Lord? What rough edges is the Master Potter working on in your life right now?

2. What "debris" could be hindering the flow of God in our churches and cities? If water flows to the place of least resistance, where is there no water because of resistance in your life?

    Pages 104-105 in *The God Chasers* explain the need to repent, request, and resist in relation to praying for cities. How can you apply these same prayer principles to your own life?

3. What can we learn about the "river" from Ezekiel Chapter 47? Can you recognize areas in your life where you are in "safe waters" but God is asking you to go deeper? Where do you need to relinquish control, grab hold of God's hand, and jump?

God Chaser Experience

If you have identified an area where you need to give up control and trust God, put visual expression to it. Stand up and confess that area to the Lord. Reach out by faith and "take His hand." Then jump. That's right. Jump. And as you jump, declare to the Lord, to yourself, and to the enemy that you are taking a leap of faith and you are putting your trust and confidence in God.

You might have read the preceding paragraph, shook your head, or laughed, and continued reading. If you have trouble with outward actions affecting spiritual conditions, take time to look at some biblical examples. (See Second Kings 13:15-19; Ezekiel 12:3-20.)

So, now stand up and jump! Go out in the deep, unfamiliar places where you must trust the Lord. Get into the "river" of His presence and swim.

Chase Him in the Word—Part A

Although it is written for you in *The God Chasers*, read the Ezekiel 47 prophecy in your own Bible, underlining words and phrases that particularly impact you. Then write a note about each text in the space provided.

Ezekiel 47:1-5

_____

_____

Ezekiel 47:9

_____

_____

Ezekiel 47:12

_____

_____

Chase Him in the Word—Part B

The following Scriptures speak symbolically of water, rain, or rivers. Briefly note key words and thoughts in the verse(s).

Psalm 42:1-2

_____

_____

John 4:10-14

_____

_____

Revelation 22:1,17

_____

_____

Zechariah 10:1; James 5:7-8

_____

_____

Hosea 10:12

_____

_____

Acts 3:19

_____

_____

John 7:37-39

_____

_____

Habakkuk 2:14

_____

_____

Chase Him in Prayer

Are you thirsty? Lift your hands and ask Him to send the rain. When you begin to feel His presence, sit or lie down and just "soak." Let waves of Living Water wash over you—cleansing and refreshing your soul. Drink deeply of the River of Life.

Don't rush this time with the Lord. Let the rain of His presence soften and minister to you.

> "Yes, Lord! Just send wave after wave of Your glory until it has literally flooded everything! May all that is not of You just be washed away downstream." *Rain*, Jesus, *reign*!
>
> Very often the "law of precedent" applies to parallel events in the natural and spiritual realms. I am so hungry for the unleashing of His glory that I can't express its intensity or urgency. So I pray,
>
> > "Lord, just let it rain! Satan is not going to have enough storm sewers to drain off the glory this time. It's going to rise so high that everybody is going to be floated off their feet and out of control in a mighty wave of the glory of God. Let it rain, Lord!"
>
> Break open the fountains of the deep. Uncap the ancient wells. Reclaim your heritage. Stake the city! The earth is the Lord's!
>
> He's done it before; He can do it again!
>
> Send the rain, Lord.
>
> *The God Chasers* page 110

CATCH Phrase—"I'm thirsty for You, Lord."

Each time throughout the day that you drink a beverage, remember the Living Water that satisfies your inner thirst and whisper to Him...

"I'm thirsty for You, Lord."

Chapter 8

The Purpose of His Presence

Divine radiation zones—presence evangelism

Time and again we ask one another, "Why can't I win my friends to the Lord? Why is it that my family members just don't seem interested in God?" The answer may shock you in its bluntness, but the truth often hurts. The reason people who know you aren't interested in your God may be because *you don't have enough of the presence of God in your life.* There is something about God's presence that makes everything else crumble in comparison. Without it, you will be just as pale and lifeless as everybody else around you. No matter what you do, without His presence, you will be "just another somebody" to those around you.

The God Chasers page 113

Chase the Key Word Through the Chapter

As you read Chapter 8, highlight or underline the word, "presence" (28 times). Include in your highlighting chase those statements that you find particularly impacting. As you read, be open to the Lord. In the midst of this study experience, He would like to *permeate your being with His presence!*

Ask Some Questions

1. How did Peter's shadow affect people? What is a "divine radiation zone"? How might this concept change our thinking about spiritual warfare?

2. Why do our evangelistic efforts, both personal and corporate, often fail? Have you ever tried to evangelize? Do you have any success stories? Why or why not?

    How can you be a "presence evangelist"?

3. What is your favorite fragrance? What is God's favorite fragrance? What attracts God? What attracts people to God?

> I encourage you to linger and soak in the presence of the Lord at every opportunity. When you draw near to Him, don't hurry and don't rush. Realize that this is (or should be) at the top of your priority list. Let God do a *deep work* in your heart and life. This is the way God creates a "deep-bored" well in your life that will become an artesian well of power and glory in His presence. *The purpose of His presence is to bring deliverance to the captives and victory to the children.*
>
> *The God Chasers* page 115

God Chaser Experience
Get close to God. Picture His arm around you as you rehearse your day. Picture yourself in your home, school, or work place shining with the fragrance of His presence.

Chase Him in the Word—Part A
Look at some of the first New Testament God chasers in the Book of Acts. Take notes about how they affected the world around them.

Acts 4:13

_____

_____

Acts 5:15-16

_____

_____

Acts 6:15

_____

_____

Chase Him in the Word—Part B

The following Scriptures speak about Jesus being seen in and through our lives. Briefly note key words and thoughts in the verse(s).

Psalm 17:15

_____

_____

Second Corinthians 3:18

_____

_____

Romans 12:2

_____

_____

Matthew 5:14-16

_____

_____

John 12:32

_____

_____

John 17:21-23

_____

_____

Second Corinthians 2:14-16

_____

_____

> ...the experience of seeing God's glory is life-changing. It is the most habit-forming experience a human being can have, and the only side effect is death to the flesh. The second reason is this: The true purpose of God's presence manifesting in our lives is *evangelism*. If we can carry a residue of God's glory back into our homes and businesses, if we can carry even a faint glow of His lingering presence into lukewarm churches, then we won't have to beg people to come to the Lord in repentance. They will run to the altar when His glory breaks their bondage (and they can't come any other way!).
>
> *The God Chasers* page 116

Chase Him in Prayer

Make a list of three people you know personally who need Jesus. Pray for them. Ask God to prepare you to meet with them. Ask God to help you shine brightly with His light into the darkness of their lives. Ask Jesus to be seen in you.

CATCH Phrase—"God chasers leave their tracks"

Every person wants to make some kind of lasting mark on the world. You will make a difference—as you carry the glory of God with you wherever you go. Today, this week, be filled with His glory, and allow Him to shine through you into the darkness of people's lives. Don't just leave "tracts." Leave tracks...leave a lasting impression of Jesus on everyone you come in contact with.

"God chasers leave their tracks"

Chapter 9

Dismantle Your Glory

The burial of man's glory is the birth of God's glory

> *My head with oil thou didst not anoint: but this woman hath anointed My feet with ointment. Wherefore I say unto thee, Her sins, which are many, are forgiven; for she loved much: but to whom little is forgiven, the same loveth little* (Luke 7:46-47).
>
> **You Must Dismantle Your Glory to Minister to Him** God spoke to me and said, "Mary dismantled her glory to minister to Me." If all the disciples were present, there were at least 12 other people in that room that day, and not one of them attained the intimacy that she obtained that day. The disciples missed it, even though they were good people like Peter, James, and John. Hear me, friend; you can be busy being a disciple and *doing the work*, but *miss the worship*!
>
> *The God Chasers* page 132

Chase the Key Word Through the Chapter
As you read Chapter 9, highlight or underline the word, "glory" (30 times). For enhanced understanding, the following is a thesaurus list for you to consider as your read the word "glory."

Magnificence	Splendor
Beauty	Grandeur
Recognition	Acclaim
Praise	Fame
Position	Status
Prestige	Honor
Self-worth	Acknowledgment
Accolade	Tribute

Ask Some Questions

1. Look at the thesaurus list above. How can we dismantle those things (our glory) in order to better minister to God?

2. We're all familiar with the story of Mary's alabaster box. Could anyone ever accuse you of extravagant worship?

    Why might the disciples have "missed" the worship in what Mary was doing?

    What are the "alabaster boxes" in your life?

3. "Son, the services that you consider your favorite services and those I favor are not the same services." When you first read that statement, what did you think?

What is the difference between entertaining man and entertaining God in a church service? How would those church services look different?

Chase Him in the Word—Part A
Study the following verses to meet some people who are sure to be in "God's Hall of Fame."

Matthew 26:10-13; Mark 14:6-9   _____

Luke 17:12-19   _____

Mark 12:42-44   _____

Genesis 5:24   _____

Psalm 51:17; Isaiah 57:15   _____

Chase Him in the Word—Part B
The following Scriptures speak about "glory." Note how each text can apply to your life.

Second Corinthians 11:30; 12:5,9

_____

_____

First Corinthians 1:29,31; Second Corinthians 10:17

_____

_____

Galatians 6:14

_____

_____

Psalm 115:1

_____

_____

Jeremiah 9:23-24

_____

_____

First Chronicles 16:10,27-29

_____

_____

First Chronicles 29:11-13

_____

_____

Chase Him in Prayer

Come to Jesus like Mary did. Kneel at His feet and pour out before Him those things in your life which you hold as precious. Pour out your gifts, talents, and ministry. Lay down your dreams, expectations, and goals. Let your own glory—your self-worth, ego, position, recognition, and acclaim—be broken in His presence.

God is saying to His people, "I will bring you close to Me *if you will dismantle your glory.*" I keep hearing Him say, "Dismantle your glory; take your ego apart and lay it aside. I don't care who you are, what you feel, or how important you think you are. I want *you,* but first you must dismantle your glory." Why? Because the burial of man's glory is often the birth of God's glory.

Mary had to get to the point where her passion made her say, "I don't care who sees me do this." You may feel a tugging and drawing in your heart as you read these words. If that is true, then I can almost guarantee that you have learned how to keep a straight face and "keep going" even though you felt like falling at the Lord's feet to ask for mercy and forgiveness. You must let your love break past the shell of "who you pretend you really are." God wants you to openly and boldly let the world know how much you really love Him—even if you have to dismantle your glory right in front of a room full of disdaining disciples.

Become a box-breaker!

Break the box of "your" precious things and finalize it by a public show of private passion.

God doesn't need your religious service; He wants your worship. And the only worship He can accept is worship that comes from humility. So if you want to see Him, you will have to dismantle your glory and bathe His feet in your tears—no matter what you may find there.

The God Chasers page 133

CATCH Phrase—"I am a BOX-BREAKER!"

Throughout your day, be conscious of things in your life that you have held precious. As situations arise that challenge your "rights" or as you feel "self" rising up inside, humble yourself and lay it all down before the Lord. Use every situation as a new opportunity to worship Him, saying, "Here it is, Lord. Here is my box of "self-worth," or "ego," or "dreams."

"I am a BOX-BREAKER!"

Chapter 10

Moses' 1,500-Year Pursuit of God's Glory

You can't seek His face and save your "face"

When we discover that God's best and deepest treasures require death to self, we often don't pursue Him any further. We don't ask the questions we need to ask to find out *why* His presence doesn't come cheaply. Perhaps it's because we think it is impertinent or we are simply afraid of His answer. Moses persisted. He had learned that *it isn't impertinent to pursue God for His own sake; it is God's greatest desire and delight.*

This burning desire to see God's glory, to see Him face to face, is one of the most important keys to revival, reformation, and the fulfillment of God's purposes on the earth. We need to look closely at the 1,500-year pursuit of God's glory by the ancient patriarch, Moses. As we noted earlier in Chapter 4, when Moses told God, "Show me Your glory," the Lord said, "You can't, Moses. Only dead men can see My face." Fortunately Moses didn't stop there. Unfortunately, the Church did.

The God Chasers page 139

Chase the Key Word Through the Chapter

As you read Chapter 10, highlight or underline the word, "face" (24 times). Include in your highlighting chase those statements that you find particularly impacting. As you read, be open to the Lord. In the midst of this study experience, He would like you to *see His face!*

Ask Some Questions

1. The hunger of one person—Moses—changed the history of a nation. What could one truly hungry person do today in a church, city, or region?

    What would a "Moses-sized" hunger look like today?

2. Can we be truly hungry without a prayer life? How is your prayer life?

3.   What does this statement mean: "Salvation is a free gift, but God's glory will cost us everything?"

We long for a Moses-style encounter without paying the price. What is the price, and how do we pay it?

4.   Read Second Corinthians 3:18. What happens to us when we do see His face? Do you want to be changed from glory to glory?

What must you do to allow that change to happen?

Chase Him in the Word—Part A

Moses had to wait 1,500 years to see His face. Christians, however, have been given unlimited access to His presence through the blood of Jesus. Read the following Scriptures and note how Jesus made a way for us to see God's glory.

Matthew 27:51; Mark 15:38; Luke 23:45

_____

_____

Hebrews 10:19-22

_____

_____

Ephesians 2:6

_____

_____

God Chaser Experience

Yes, Moses had to wait 1,500 years to see His face; but you, dear God chaser, are invited to boldly enter His throne room! Second Corinthians 3:18 tells us that as we behold His glory, we are changed. We cannot change ourselves. It is only in His presence that we are transformed...from one degree of glory to the next.

Spend time in His presence. Choose a time and place where there will be no distractions. Come boldly, and with full assurance, seeing yourself as the person God's Word declares you to be...forgiven and cleansed...seated there with Him in heavenly places.

Tell Him how much you love Him. Don't seek His hand—don't bring out your prayer list. Just allow yourself to love and be loved by Pappa God...and you will be changed.

Chase Him in the Word—Part B

The following Scriptures speak of God's glory and of His face. Briefly note key words and thoughts in the verse(s).

Psalm 27:8

_____

_____

Second Chronicles 7:14

_____

_____

Exodus 33:12-15, 18-23

_____

_____

Luke 9:28-34

_____

_____

Second Corinthians 3:14-18

_____

_____

Ephesians 1:13-18

_____

_____

Revelation 22:4-5

_____

_____

Chase Him in Prayer

Pray from the position of one who is seated with Him in heavenly places. Ask God what is on His heart. Ask Him to show you people from His perspective, and pray accordingly.

He will not frustrate us. God will allow Himself to be caught by us. As a father playing tag with his child allows himself to be caught by the laughing, loving child, so too will the heavenly Father allow Himself to be caught. In fact, just when you would tire in despair, He will turn and catch you. He wants to be "captured" by our love. He eagerly awaits the laughing, loving encounter. He has missed those times with man since the Garden. Intuitively, God chasers have known this. *They were willing to chase the "uncatchable," knowing the "impossible" would catch them.* In fact, one famous God chaser wrote this:

> *I follow after, if that I may apprehend* that for which also I am apprehended of Christ Jesus (Philippians 3:12b).

Paul caught Him!
So can you! Come join the company of God chasers!
The "chase" is on...

The God Chasers page 151

CATCH Phrase—"I am a God chaser"

After you have seen His glory, nothing in this world will ever again bring the same kind of satisfaction. Nothing this life offers can compare to being in His presence. Acts 17:28 says that we live and move and have our being in Him.

Live that way! In every situation, amidst every crisis and problem, as well as in the sweet times of communion with your heavenly Father, declare...

"Blessings as you continue your chase!"

Concluding Thoughts

Spiritual truth can never be fully attained in a classroom or church meeting setting. It must be integrated into the experiences of life. The environment into which the seed of the Word falls will determine the nature of the fruit that is produced by that Word. Faith is the proper environment for the growth of spiritual truth in the soul of man.

To experience the ultimate benefit from this study guide, we encourage you to take these cherished truths and allow the Holy Spirit to work them into the very fabric of your being. Receive them into your spirit, allow them to penetrate your heart, mind, and soul, meditate upon them, and seek the Holy Spirit's help in applying them to every facet of your life. As these truths are growing in you they will be accompanied by your own personal experiences. Then, watered by the outworking of obedience to the Divine will, the seeds will yield their own harvest of spiritual fruit.

Lastly, our learning is not simply for us to experience the truth only for ourselves. It is our responsibility to allow the truth to bring us into Divine alignment with the purposes of God so that we can teach and bless others. As the Word is worked into your life, the Lord will give you words to accurately and powerfully transfer these truths to others.

GodChasers.network is the ministry of Tommy and Jeannie Tenney. Their heart's desire and ministry mandate is unifying the Body of Christ and pursuing the presence of God—not just in churches, but in cities and communities all over the world.

How to contact us:

By Mail:

GodChasers.network
P.O. Box 3355
Pineville, Louisiana 71361
USA

By Phone:

Voice:	318.44CHASE (318.442.4273)
Fax:	318.442.6884
Orders:	888.433.3355

By Internet:

E-mail:	GodChaser@GodChasers.net
Website:	www.GodChasers.net

 # *Join Today*

When you join the **GodChasers.network** we'll send you a free teaching tape and our ministry letter!

If you share in our vision for personal and corporate revival and want to stay current on how the Lord is using GodChasers.network, please add your name to our ministry list. We'd like to keep you updated on the fires of revival being set around the world through Tommy and the GodChasers team! We'll also send schedule updates and make you aware of new resources as they become available.

Run with us by calling or writing to:

Tommy Tenney
GodChasers.network
P.O. Box 3355
Pineville, Louisiana 71361-3355
USA

318-44CHASE (318.442.4273)
or sign up online at www.GodChasers.net/lists/

We regret that we are only able to send regular postal mailings to U.S. residents at this time. If you live outside the U.S. you can still add your postal address to our mailing list—you will automatically begin to receive our mailings as soon as they are available in your area.

E-mail Announcement List

If you'd like to receive information from us via e-mail, just provide an e-mail address when you contact us and let us know that you want to be included on the e-mail announcement list!

Chase God With Us
Daily E-mail Bible Reading Program
An Invitation to Run

If you already have a daily Bible reading plan, we commend you. If you don't we invite you to join with us in reading God's Word. Just go to our website @www.godchasers.net and click on Chase God to sign up and you will start receiving the daily reading! It only takes a few minutes each day to read the Bible in a year. Just find today's date and continue faithfully for the next twelve months.

If you skip a day, don't get discouraged. Don't let minor setbacks become major obstacles. Remember that the goal isn't to follow a "schedule" religiously; the goal is to spend time with God in His Word.

If you find yourself missing days fequently and are tempted to give up altogether, Don't! Disregard the dates and simply read a portion whenever you can. You may not feel like you're making progress, but as you move forward through more and more of the readings, you'll see how far you're really getting and be encouraged to continue.

God Chasers Ministry Internship

I'm excited to announce a brand new GodChasers Internship Program for teenagers and young adults. I want to train the next generation of GodChasers so they can pass on this passion to their friends and communities! This year-long program will include classroom time, practical application and an opportunity to accompany my traveling team on a ministry trip. This isn't a summer camp or vacation—it will be hard work. It will involve a lot of sacrifice. Participants will be challenged and stretched and taken far beyond their comfort zones. It will be an intense, no-nonsense, power-packed time. Real work! Real ministry! Real destiny!

Tony

AUDIOTAPE ALBUMS BY

Tommy Tenney

FANNING THE FLAMES
(audiotape album) $20 plus $4.50 S&H

Tape 1 — The Application of the Blood and the Ark of the Covenant: Most of the churches in America today dwell in an outer-court experience. Jesus made atonement with His own blood, once for all, and the veil in the temple was rent from top to bottom.

Tape 2 — A Tale of Two Cities—Nazareth & Nineveh: What city is more likely to experience revival: Nazareth or Nineveh? You might be surprised....

Tape 3 — The "I" Factor: Examine the difference between *ikabod* and *kabod* ("glory"). The arm of flesh cannot achieve what needs to be done. God doesn't need us; we need Him.

KEYS TO LIVING THE REVIVED LIFE
(audiotape album) $20 plus $4.50 S&H

Tape 1 - Fear Not: To have no fear is to have faith, and that perfect love casts out fear, so we establish the trust of a child in our loving Father.

Tape 2 - Hanging in There: Have you ever been tempted to give up, quit, and throw in the towel? This message is a word of encouragement for you.

Tape 3 - Fire of God: Fire purges the sewer of our souls and destroys the hidden things that would cause disease. Learn the way out of a repetitive cycle of seasonal times of failure.

NEW!
WHAT'S THE FIGHT ABOUT?
(audiotape album) $20 plus $4.50 S&H

Tape 1 - Preserving the Family: God's special gift to the world is the family. If we don't preserve the family, the Church is one generation from extinction. God's desire is to heal the wounds of the family from the inside out.

Tape 2 - Unity in the Body: An examination of the levels of Unity that must be respected and achieved before "Father, let them be one" becomes an answered prayer!

Tape 3 - What's the Fight About?: If you're throwing dirt, you're just loosing ground! In **What's the Fight About?** Tommy invades our backyards to help us discover our differences aren't so different after all!

TURNING ON THE LIGHT OF THE GLORY
(video) $20 plus $4.50 S&H

Tommy deals with turning on the light of the glory and presence of God, and he walks us through the necessary process and ingredients to potentially unleash what His Body has always dreamed of.

THREE NEW VIDEOS BY

Tommy Tenney

LET'S BUILD A BONFIRE VOL. 1:
LET IT FALL

(video) $20 plus $4.50 S&H

One hour of the best worship and word
from the GodChaser gatherings.

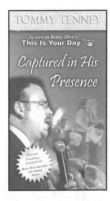

CAPTURED IN
HIS PRESENCE

(1 hour video)
$25 plus $4.50 S&H

An encounter with God captured on tape as
seen on *This Is Your Day* with Benny Hinn.

FOLLOW THE MAN
ON THE COLT

(1 hour video) $20 plus $4.50 S&H

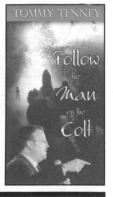

Are you too proud to ride with Him? Humility
is the catalyst that will move your answers
from a crawl to a walk to a run and to a ride.

Tommy Tenney has touched the heart of a generation who crave for an encounter with their Lord.
The passion of his heart, captured in his writings, has
ignited a flame of godly pursuit across this world.

The Daily Chase offers you the best of those writings. Each day there awaits you a fresh encounter with
the One you long for. Don't hold anything back.

Sample God Chaser Worship CD* enclosed in back of
book includes:

• Sample songs from Jeannie Tenney's album "Holy Hunger"

• Sample songs from a NEW God Chaser worship album

• Sample video clips from the accompanying music video

*1st printing only

Elegant Case Bound Edition, $19.00

5 TT

Run With Us!

Become a GodChasers Monthly Revival Partner

Two men, a farmer and his friend, were looking out over the farmer's fields one afternoon. It was a beautiful sight—it was nearly harvest time, and the wheat was swaying gently in the wind. Inspired by this idyllic scene, the friend said, "Look at God's provision!" The farmer replied, "You should have seen it when God had it by Himself!"

This humorous story illustrates a serious truth. Every good and perfect gift comes from Him: but we are supposed to be more than just passive recipients of His grace and blessings. We must never forget that only God can cause a plant to grow—*but it is equally important to remember that we are called to do our part in the sowing, watering, and harvesting.*

When you sow seed into this ministry, you help us reach people and places you could never imagine. The faithful support of individuals like you allows us to send resources, free of charge, to many who would otherwise be unable to obtain them. Your gifts help us carry the Gospel all over the world—including countries that have been closed to evangelism. Would you prayerfully consider becoming a revival partner with us? As a small token of our gratitude, our Revival Partners who send a monthly gift of $20 or more receive a teaching tape and ministry letter every month. This ministry could not survive without the faithful support of partners like you!

Stand with me now—so we can run together later!

In Hot Pursuit,

Tommy Tenney
& The GodChasers.network Staff

Become a Monthly Revival Partner by calling or writing to:

Tommy Tenney/GodChasers.network
P.O. Box 3355
Pineville, Louisiana 71361-3355
318.44CHASE (318.442.4273)

Additional copies of this book and other
book titles from DESTINY IMAGE are
available at your local bookstore.

For a complete list of our titles,
visit us at www.destinyimage.com
Send a request for a catalog to:

Destiny Image® Publishers, Inc.
P.O. Box 310
Shippensburg, PA 17257-0310

*"Speaking to the Purposes of God for This
Generation and for the Generations to Come"*

Disappoint will be
DIVINE Appointm

NEW Dimension of Unseen
NOW! Logos and
Rhema
FAVOR of GOD
IN negotiation
UNPREDICTABLE
UNUSUAL